Life on the Farm

by Teddy Borth

ABDO
ON THE FARM
Kids

www.abdopublishing.com

Published by Abdo Kids, a division of ABDO, PO Box 398166, Minneapolis, Minnesota 55439.

Copyright © 2015 by Abdo Consulting Group, Inc. International copyrights reserved in all countries. No part of this book may be reproduced in any form without written permission from the publisher.

Printed in the United States of America, North Mankato, Minnesota.

052014

092014

Photo Credits: Glow Images, Shutterstock, Thinkstock

Production Contributors: Teddy Borth, Jennie Forsberg, Grace Hansen

Design Contributors: Candice Keimig, Laura Rask, Dorothy Toth

Library of Congress Control Number: 2013952563

Cataloging-in-Publication Data

Borth, Teddy.

 Life on the farm / Teddy Borth.

   p. cm. -- (On the farm)

ISBN 978-1-62970-053-3 (lib. bdg.)

Includes bibliographical references and index.

1. Farm life--Juvenile literature. 2. Family life--Juvenile literature. I. Title.

630--dc23

            2013952563

Table of Contents

Life on the Farm

Farmers have chores on the farm. Chores are done every day.

4

5

Gather Eggs

Chickens lay eggs.

Eggs need to be gathered.

Groom Horses

Horses are brushed.

Horses are cleaned.

Milk Cows

Cows are **milked** at

least twice a day.

Feed Animals

All the animals need food. Farmers fill the feed box with food.

13

Fill Water

All the animals need

water. Farmers carry

water to the animals.

Check the Fences

Fences are checked.

Fences keep animals

from getting lost.

16

Garden

The garden is watered.

Vegetables are picked

from the garden.

Clean

Chicken nests are cleaned.

Horse stalls are cleaned.

More Facts

- Children as young as 2 years old help with chores on the farm.

- Most farmers start their day at 4:00 am!

- Kids living on farms wake up early to do their chores, go to school, and come home to help with more work on the farm.

- The **average** horse eats about 25 pounds (11.3 kg) of hay each day!

Glossary

average – the usual; typical; standard.

gather – to take from scattered places and bring together.

milk – to draw milk from a cow's udder.

Index

abdokids.com

Use this code to log on to abdokids.com and access crafts, games, videos and more!

Abdo Kids Code:
OLK0533